The Hymns We Love

DANIEL PARTNER

BARBOUR
PUBLISHING

The Hymns We Love

© 2003 by Barbour Publishing, Inc.

ISBN 1-58660-738-3

Cover image © PhotoDisc

Selections included are taken from *Hymns of Devotion, Hymns of God's Love, Hymns of Peace,* and *Hymns of Worship,* all written by Daniel Partner, © 2001 by Barbour Publishing, Inc.

Published by Barbour Publishing, Inc., P.O. Box 719, Uhrichsville, Ohio 44683, www.barbourbooks.com

ecpa Member of the
Evangelical Christian
Publishers Association

Printed in the United States of America.
5 4 3 2 1

Hymns of Devotion—

Take My Life and Let It Be 9
Just As I Am 16
I Need Thee Every Hour 22

Hymns of God's Love—

Amazing Grace 31
Love Divine, All Loves Excelling 39
When I Survey the Wondrous
    Cross 45

Hymns of Peace—

Nearer, Still Nearer 55
O God, Our Help in Ages Past 61
Rock of Ages 68

Hymns of Worship—

For the Beauty of the Earth 77
Come Thou Almighty King 82
All Hail the Power of Jesus' Name . . .88

Hymns of Devotion

TAKE MY LIFE AND LET IT BE

Take my life, and let it be consecrated, Lord,
　　to Thee.
Take my moments and my days; let them
　　flow in ceaseless praise.
Take my hands, and let them move at the
　　impulse of Thy love.
Take my feet, and let them be swift and
　　beautiful for Thee.

Take my voice, and let me sing always, only,
　　for my King.
Take my lips, and let them be filled with
　　messages from Thee.
Take my silver and my gold; not a mite would
　　I withhold.
Take my intellect, and use every power as
　　Thou shalt choose.

Take my will, and make it Thine; it shall be
　　no longer mine.
Take my heart, it is Thine own; it shall be
　　Thy royal throne.
Take my love, my Lord, I pour at Thy feet
　　its treasure store.
Take myself, and I will be ever, only,
　　all for Thee.

And so,

dear brothers and sisters,

I plead with you to give

your bodies to God.

Let them be a living

and holy sacrifice—

the kind he will accept.

When you think of

what he has done for you,

is this too much to ask?

ROMANS 12:1

I went [to Areley House] for a little visit of five days," recalled Frances Havergal. "There were ten persons in the house, some unconverted and long prayed for, some converted, but not rejoicing Christians. [The Lord] gave me the prayer, 'Lord, give me all in this house!' And he just did. Before I left the house, every one had got a blessing. The last night of my visit after I had retired, the governess asked me to go to the two daughters. They were crying. Then and there both of them trusted and rejoiced; it was nearly midnight. I was too happy to sleep and passed most of the night in praise and renewal of my own consecration; and these little couplets formed themselves, and chimed in my heart one after another till they finished with 'Ever, only, all for Thee!' "

Those are the final words of Havergal's cherished hymn. With the first lines she sings, "Take my life and let it be consecrated, Lord to Thee." The word *consecrated* means devoted entirely, dedicated. Havergal goes on to list everything she desires the Lord to take— moments and days, hands and feet, voice and lips, silver and gold, intellect and will, heart and love—a very complete list. Its sum: her entire self.

The key word in this hymn is *take*. Havergal is submitting herself to God. She is simply making herself available to God. She is simply making herself available for the divine purpose. She is not insisting;

she is not presumptuous. No one can demand to be used by God. The best we can do is be available to God, praying, "Take me."

Frances R. Havergal was born in Worcestershire, England, and educated there and in Düsseldorf, Germany. She wrote many hymns that emphasize faith, devotion, and service to God. She was a master of several languages, including Latin, Hebrew, Greek, French, and German. She was a natural musician with a pleasing, well-trained voice and a brilliant hand at the piano. This extraordinary woman was also a devoted Bible student who memorized large sections of Scripture. She practiced a disciplined prayer life and noted in her Bible the times and topics of her prayers. She described her way of writing hymns this way: "Writing is praying with me, for I never seem to write even a verse by myself, and feel like a little child writing; you know a child would look up at every sentence and say, 'And what shall I say next?' That is just what I do; I ask that at every line He would give me not merely thoughts and power, but also every word, even the very rhymes. Very often I have a most distinct and happy consciousness of direct answers."

She is called the "consecration poet" because her hymns often emphasize one's complete dedication to God. Significantly, her namesake is Nicholas Ridley, a prominent Bishop martyred at Oxford in 1555.

Although she died 120 years ago, Havergal's hymns are still loved and sung today. Other hymns by Frances Havergal include "Who Is on the Lord's Side?", "Thou Art Coming, O My Savior," and "I Am Trusting Thee, Lord Jesus." A volume of her verse, entitled *Poetical Works*, was published in 1884. Her prose writings include *Kept for the Master's Use* and *Royal Commandments and Royal Bounty*.

Lord, take my will; make it yours,

and it will not be mine anymore.

Take my heart; it is yours.

Make it into your throne.

Take my love, Lord; it is my only treasure.

I pour it at your feet.

And I pray that one day

you will take my entire self.

Then I will be ever, only, and all for you.

One of the Pharisees asked Jesus

to come to his home for a meal,

so Jesus accepted the invitation

and sat down to eat.

A certain immoral woman heard

he was there and brought a beautiful jar

filled with expensive perfume.

Then she knelt behind him

at his feet, weeping.

Her tears fell on his feet,

and she wiped them off with her hair.

Then she kept kissing his feet and

putting perfume on them.

LUKE 7:36–38

JUST AS I AM

Just as I am, without one plea,
But that Thy blood was shed for me,
And that Thou bidst me come to Thee,
O Lamb of God, I come, I come.

Just as I am, and waiting not
To rid my soul of one dark blot,
To Thee whose blood can cleanse each spot,
O Lamb of God, I come, I come.

Just as I am, though tossed about
With many a conflict, many a doubt,
Fightings and fears within, without,
O Lamb of God, I come, I come.

Just as I am, poor, wretched, blind;
Sight, riches, healing of the mind,
Yea, all I need in Thee to find,
O Lamb of God, I come, I come.

Have mercy on me, O God,

because of your unfailing love.

Because of your great compassion,

blot out the stain of my sins.

Wash me clean from my guilt.

Purify me from my sin.

PSALM 51:1–2

Charlotte Elliott's brother was a Christian minister. Here is what he said about the hymn "Just As I Am": "In the course of a long ministry, I hope I have been permitted to see some of the fruit of my labor, but I feel that far more has been done by a single hymn of my sister's."

Elliott's hymn contains the same message as does a story told about two men who went up to the temple to pray. One was a Pharisee and the other a tax collector. "The proud Pharisee stood by himself and prayed this prayer: 'I thank you, God, that I am not a sinner like everyone else, especially like that tax collector over there! For I never cheat, I don't sin, I don't commit adultery, I fast twice a week, and I give you a tenth of my income.'

"But the tax collector stood at a distance and dared not even lift his eyes to heaven as he prayed. Instead, he beat his chest in sorrow, saying, 'O God, be merciful to me, for I am a sinner'" (Luke 18:11–13).

Jesus tells the lesson of his story—"I tell you, this sinner, not the Pharisee, returned home justified before God. For the proud will be humbled, but the humble will be honored" (Luke 18:14).

One of these men was humble, the other was self-exalting. What was the Pharisee so exultant about? His own goodness. Why was the tax collector so humble? He knew he was a sinner. In fact, they were both sinners, but only one admitted it.

If you think you must be on your best behavior to come to God, remember this: Your best is not good enough. Jesus said, "No one is good but God alone" (Mark 10:18 RSV). God is not like Santa Claus who, as the old poem says, keeps a list of naughty and nice. God has no need of such a list since "all have sinned; all fall short of God's glorious standard" (Romans 3:23).

No amount of self-improvement can bring you to the level of God. For this reason everyone must sing, "Just as I am, without one plea, but that your blood was shed for me, and that you bid me come to Thee, O Lamb of God, I come, I come!"

The hymn was written after Charlotte Elliott heard the truth of the gospel from the Swiss evangelist Cèsar Malan. She not only believed in Jesus, she wrote this most popular of gospel hymns. For twenty-five years, Elliott was editor of the annual *Christian Remembrancer Pocketbook*, and she assisted in the publication of the *Invalid's Hymn Book*, which contained 112 of her poems. She wrote 150 hymns that address the concerns of those in sickness and sorrow.

Dear Lord,

save me from being

haughty like the praying

Pharisee and let me know your

love as you receive me just as I am.

But now you belong to Christ Jesus.

Though you once were far away from God,

now you have been brought near to him

because of the blood of Christ.

EPHESIANS 2:13

I NEED THEE EVERY HOUR

I need Thee every hour, most gracious Lord;
No tender voice like Thine can peace afford.

I need Thee every hour, stay Thou nearby;
Temptations lose their power when Thou
    art nigh.

I need Thee every hour, in joy or pain;
Come quickly and abide, or life is in vain.

I need Thee every hour; teach me Thy will;
And Thy rich promises in me fulfill.

Refrain
I need Thee, O I need Thee;
Every hour I need Thee;
O bless me now, my Savior,
I come to Thee.

As the deer pants

for streams of water,

so I long for you, O God.

I thirst for God, the living God.

When can I come and stand before him?

Day and night,

I have only tears for food,

while my enemies continually taunt me,

saying,

"Where is this God of yours?"

PSALM 42:1–3

Annie Sherwood Hawks wrote the lyrics for "I Need Thee Every Hour." Her poems first began being published when she was fourteen years old. She eventually wrote four hundred hymns; most of them were for use in Sunday schools. She married in 1857, lived in Brooklyn, New York, and attended the Hanson Place Baptist Church. There, Robert Lowry, who wrote the score for "I Need Thee Every Hour," was the pastor.

This hymn expresses the heart of a real seeker of God. There is such a seeker in the poetry of the Song of Solomon, an astounding scriptural account of love between a young man and woman. "I sought him whom my soul loves," says the young woman. "I sought him, but found him not; I called him, but he gave no answer" (3:1 NRSV). This is a common experience of believers, seekers, and lovers of Christ. Simply put, it is the experience of "Where did he go?" Annie Hawks probably experienced it. Have you?

There was a sixteenth-century Spanish Roman Catholic reformer, mystic, and poet named John of the Cross. He wrote a classic of world literature— *Dark Night of the Soul.* John knew the experience of seeking yet not finding the Lord. The following is a paraphrase of a portion of his book about the Song of Solomon, *Commentary of the Spiritual Canticle:*

I sought him but I did not find him (see Song of Solomon 3:1). You ask: Since the one I love is within me, why don't I find him or experience him?

Here is the reason: He remains concealed because you do not also hide yourself in order to meet and experience him. Anyone who wants to find a hidden treasure must enter the hiding place secretly. Then she will be hidden just as the treasure is hidden. To find him, forget all your possessions and all creation and hide in the interior, secret chamber of your spirit. There, closing the door behind you, pray to your Father in secret (see Matthew 6:6). Hidden with him you will experience him in hiding; love and enjoy him in hiding. You will delight with him in a way transcending all language and feeling.

The secret place John of the Cross is talking about is very hard to describe. The Bible resorts to poetic images in the Song of Solomon, the Psalms, and elsewhere to describe the place where our relationship with God is realized.

Here is what Jesus said about it: "I am the true vine, and my Father is the gardener. Remain in me, and I will remain in you. For a branch cannot produce fruit if it is severed from the vine, and you cannot be fruitful apart from me. Yes, I am the vine; you are the branches. Those who remain in me, and I in them, will produce much fruit. For apart from me you can do nothing" (John 15:1, 4–5).

The hiding place where a believer can love and enjoy God is like the very spot where a branch is connected to a vine. There the flow of the life of the vine enters the branch. This is why Jesus advised, "When you pray, go away by yourself, shut the door behind you, and pray to your Father secretly. Then your Father, who knows all secrets, will reward you" (Matthew 6:6).

O God, give me grace

to forget all my possessions

and all the rest of creation.

Show me where and how

to hide in the interior,

secret chamber of my spirit

where the flow of the vine

enters the branch.

Let me experience

you in this way.

Bend down, O Lord,

and hear my prayer;

answer me, for I need your help.

Protect me, for I am devoted to you.

Save me, for I serve you and trust you.

You are my God.

Be merciful, O Lord,

for I am calling on you constantly.

Give me happiness, O Lord,

for my life depends on you.

PSALM 86:1–4

Hymns of God's Love

AMAZING GRACE

Amazing grace! How sweet the sound
That saved a wretch like me!
I once was lost, but now am found;
Was blind, but now I see.

'Twas grace that taught my heart to fear,
And grace my fears relieved;
How precious did that grace appear
The hour I first believed.

Through many dangers, toils and snares,
I have already come;
'Tis grace hath brought me safe thus far,
And grace will lead me home.

The Lord has promised good to me,
His Word my hope secures;
He will my Shield and Portion be,
As long as life endures.

Yea, when this flesh and heart shall fail,
And mortal life shall cease,
I shall possess, within the veil,
A life of joy and peace.

The earth shall soon dissolve like snow,
The sun forbear to shine;
But God, Who called me here below,
Shall be forever mine.

When we've been there ten thousand years,
Bright shining as the sun,
We've no less days to sing God's praise
Than when we'd first begun.

I know this:

I was blind, and now I can see!

JOHN 9:25

I was raised in a good, churchgoing family, yet I never heard the hymn "Amazing Grace" sung in church. I find this amazing in itself, since it is possibly the most-played hymn in America. I first heard it sung by the pop singer Judy Collins—which for me is ironic, since Judy Collins and I attended the same church when I was a child. I don't remember, but I'm told she played the piano there. Maybe she played "Amazing Grace"—I can't say. Anyway, I left the church and went on my way and finally heard the beautiful words of this song somewhere far out in the world.

Eventually grace appeared to me in the hour I first believed, just as it did to John Newton, the author of this and many other hymns. Newton was also the author of the epitaph for his own gravestone.

Here's what it says:

> *JOHN NEWTON, Clerk*
> *Once an infidel and libertine*
> *A servant of slaves in Africa,*
> *Was, by the rich mercy of our*
> *Lord and Savior JESUS CHRIST,*
> *restored, pardoned, and appointed to preach*
> *the Gospel which he had long labored to destroy.*
> *He ministered,*
> *Near sixteen years in Olney, in Bucks,*
> *And twenty-eight years in this Church.*

Newton was born in 1725 in London, England. After two years of schooling, he went to sea with his father. He was eleven years old. His life seems to have been as amazing as his hymn—that of a reckless, debauched seaman. He was once flogged as a deserter and was himself deserted on the shores of Africa. There, he was enslaved for fifteen months. In 1748, Newton was piloting a waterlogged ship on a storm-plagued voyage from Africa to England. He thought his end was near. That was when grace began to teach his heart to fear.

He remained at sea and became captain of a ship working in the slave trade. In 1854, Newton returned to England to stay. He worked as a clerk in the surveyor's office of the Port of Liverpool. Newton studied Hebrew and Greek, became acquainted with the religious leaders John Whitefield and John Wesley, and was eventually ordained in the Church of England. He became curate at Olney, Bucks, in 1764. There he formed a lifelong friendship with William Cowper, author of "God Moves in a Mysterious Way" and many other hymns. The two wrote and published the *Olney Hymns*, which included "Amazing Grace." John Newton's autobiography, *An Authentic Narrative*, was published in 1764.

How is it possible for a man to be drawn out of such a life and become such a gift to the church and the world? His mother had died when he was a child; so who prayed for John Newton? Apparently, someone did.

I know that grace appeared to me because of the prayers of my mother and others in the Women's Society of Christian Service at the Wheat Ridge Methodist Church. My experience of amazing grace compels me to persist in prayer for my own children.

Lord, I know that someday

my flesh and heart will fail,

my mortal life shall cease.

But I thank you that I possess your

invisible life of joy and peace.

The earth will soon dissolve like snow,

and the sun refuse to shine.

But I worship you because

I know you are forever mine.

Come and listen,

all you who fear God,

and I will tell you what

he did for me.

PSALM 66:16

LOVE DIVINE,
ALL LOVES EXCELLING

Love divine, all loves excelling,
Joy of heaven to earth come down;
Fix in us Thy humble dwelling;
All Thy faithful mercies crown!
Jesus, Thou art all compassion,
Pure unbounded love Thou art;
Visit us with Thy salvation;
Enter every trembling heart.

Breathe, O breathe Thy loving Spirit,
Into every troubled breast!
Let us all in Thee inherit;
Let us find that second rest.
Take away our bent to sinning;
Alpha and Omega be;
End of faith, as its Beginning,
Set our hearts at liberty.

We know how much

God loves us,

and we have put our trust in him.

God is love,

and all who live in love live in God,

and God lives in them.

1 JOHN 4:16

The author of this hymn, Charles Wesley, and his brother John were sons of Samuel Wesley, a Church of England cleric, and his devout and capable wife Susanna. They attended Oxford University, followed their father's footsteps into the ministry, and became the founders of the Methodist Church.

While at Oxford, Charles Wesley studied classical literature. As it turned out, he became a significant figure in English literature— "Love Divine, All Loves Excelling" is one of the more than three thousand hymns written by Wesley. John Dryden (1631–1700) is among Wesley's fellow poets. In fact, Wesley probably copied the pattern of rhyme and meter in "Love Divine, All Loves Excelling" from Dryden's poem about Camelot titled "King Arthur." The similarity is clearly seen: "Fairest Isle, all isles excelling, seats of pleasure and of love," wrote Dryden. "Love divine, all loves excelling, joy of heaven to earth come down," sang Wesley.

While Dryden wrote of King Arthur's legendary kingdom, Wesley focused on Jesus Christ's heavenly kingdom. Arthur's is fantasy; Christ's is reality. From the first line of his hymn, Wesley outlines some features of the heavenly kingdom that are probably recognizable to people who believe.

The coming of the kingdom began with the incarnation of Jesus Christ—the birth of God in humanity:

"Love divine, all loves excelling, joy of heaven to earth come down." The kingdom is established as Christ makes his home in the hearts of believers: "Fix in us Thy humble dwelling; All Thy faithful mercies crown!" Since God has begun the work of settling the kingdom on earth, Wesley prays that Christ would finish the work: "Alpha and Omega be; end of faith, as its beginning, set our hearts at liberty."

Next comes a prayer for Christ's return—for the physical manifestation of the Kingdom of God. "Suddenly return and never, never more Thy temples leave" is the poet's eloquent plea before he describes a view of the kingdom's bliss:

> *Thee we would be always blessing,*
> *Serve Thee as Thy hosts above,*
> *Pray and praise Thee without ceasing,*
> *Glory in Thy perfect love.*

As a minister in the Church of England, Charles Wesley led worshipers in the Lord's Prayer. Many Christians frequently repeat the familiar words of Matthew 6:9–13. With his hymn "Love Divine, All Loves Excelling," Wesley had found a fresh way to utter the hope of all the ages—"Your kingdom come. Your will be done, on earth as it is in heaven" (v. 10 NRSV). "Finish, then, Thy new creation," the hymn writer says. "Pure and spotless let us be. Let us see Thy great salvation perfectly restored in Thee. Changed from glory into glory, till in heaven we take our place, till we cast our crowns before Thee, lost in wonder, love, and praise."

Jesus, Lord, I pray for that moment when the last trumpet sounds, when the dead are raised imperishable and my mortal body puts on immortality, when death is swallowed up in your victory, and the Kingdom of God is seen on this earth.

Then I saw a new heaven

and a new earth,

for the old heaven and the old earth

had disappeared.

And the sea was also gone.

And I saw the holy city,

the new Jerusalem,

coming down from God

out of heaven like a beautiful bride

prepared for her husband.

REVELATION 21:1–2

WHEN I SURVEY
THE WONDROUS CROSS

When I survey the wondrous cross
On which the Prince of glory died,
My richest gain I count but loss,
And pour contempt on all my pride.

Forbid it, Lord, that I should boast,
Save in the death of Christ my God!
All the vain things that charm me most,
I sacrifice them to His blood.

See from His head, His hands, His feet,
Sorrow and love flow mingled down!
Did e'er such love and sorrow meet,
Or thorns compose so rich a crown?

As for me,

God forbid that I should boast

about anything except the cross

of our Lord Jesus Christ.

Because of that cross,

my interest in this world died long ago,

and the world's interest in me

is also long dead.

GALATIANS 6:14

It is an understatement to say that Isaac Watts was a precocious child. He learned Latin at age five, Greek at nine, French at eleven, and when he was twelve he mastered Hebrew. His habit of spontaneously making rhymes as he spoke drove his father to distraction. Watts grew up to be an Nonconformist cleric and eventually wrote over six hundred hymns. Today he is known as the father of English hymnody.

Watts wrote "When I Survey the Wondrous Cross" when he was thirty-four years old. British poet Matthew Arnold (1822–1888) called it the greatest hymn in the English language. This is high praise coming as it does from the preeminent literary critic of the nineteenth century who occupied the chair of poetry at Oxford University.

The hymn's powerful images and strong emotion combine with its author's pure devotion to God. The blend is a strengthening tonic for a believer's faith. Watts wrote the hymn as he was preparing to take Communion, an event central to the Christian faith because it memorializes Christ's work of redemption through his death on the cross—the single most significant act in human history.

Isaac Watts presided over the service of the Lord's Table as pastor of Mark Lane Independent [Congregational] Chapel, London, from 1699 until his health declined in 1712. Here Watts wrote and published most of his hymns. As he served the Eucharist, the young minister may have said words similar to these:

> *On the night he was handed over to suffer-*
> *ing and death, our Lord Jesus Christ took bread;*
> *and when he had given thanks, he broke it, and*
> *gave it to his disciples, and said, "Take, eat: This*
> *is my body which is given for you. Do this for*
> *the remembrance of me."*
>
> *After supper he took the cup of wine; and*
> *when he had given thanks, he gave it to them,*
> *and said, "Drink this, all of you: This is my*
> *blood of the new covenant, which is shed for*
> *you and for many for the forgiveness of sins.*
> *Whenever you drink it, do this for the remem-*
> *brance of me."*
>
> *Therefore we proclaim the mystery of faith:*
> *Christ has died. Christ is risen. Christ will come*
> *again.**

The second verse of this moving hymn expresses the centrality of the death of Jesus Christ in a believer's life:

> *Forbid it, Lord, that I should boast,*
> *Save in the death of Christ my God!*

All the vain things that charm me most,
I sacrifice them to His blood.

The Communion service is a reminder of the vast importance of Christ's death. Isaac Watts said that Christ's death expresses "Love so amazing, so divine." It is really beyond words. Yet the words of Watts's hymn "When I Survey the Wondrous Cross" are his superb attempt to express the immense mystery of Christ's crucifixion.

* *The Book of Common Prayer.* New York: The Church Hymnal Corporation, 1979. pp. 362–63.

Lord, when my heart

sees the wondrous cross on which you died,

I have to count everything I have as loss

and pour contempt on all my pride.

Lord, don't let me boast about

anything except your death.

I sacrifice all the vain things

that charm me most to your blood.

Carrying the

cross by himself,

Jesus went to the place

called Skull Hill

(in Hebrew, Golgotha).

There they crucified him.

JOHN 19:17–18

Hymns of Peace

NEARER, STILL NEARER

Nearer, still nearer, close to Thy heart,
Draw me, my Savior—so precious Thou art!
Fold me, oh, fold me close to Thy breast.
Shelter me safe in that "Haven of Rest";
Shelter me safe in that "Haven of Rest."

Nearer, still nearer, nothing I bring,
Naught as an off'ring to Jesus, my King;
Only my sinful, now contrite heart.
Grant me the cleansing Thy blood doth impart.
Grant me the cleansing Thy blood doth impart.

Nearer, still nearer, Lord, to be Thine!
Sin, with its follies, I gladly resign,
All of its pleasures, pomp and its pride,
Give me but Jesus, my Lord, crucified.
Give me but Jesus, my Lord, crucified.

Draw close to God,

and God will draw close to you.

Wash your hands,

you sinners;

purify your hearts,

you hypocrites.

JAMES 4:8

"Fold me, oh, fold me close to Thy breast," Leila Morris prays, "shelter me safe in that haven of rest." Her sweet hymn brings to mind the above verse from the Epistle of James in the New Testament. At first, I thought I'd quote only the first sentence of this verse because its second sentence is so harsh. "Wash your hands you sinners. . ." seems to ruin the sentiment of "Draw close to God. . ." But instead of ruining it, the second sentence of James 4:8 tells how it is actually possible to come close to God.

The Christian gospel points out an uncomfortable fact: Humanity is separated from God. The separation is called sin and it causes us to sin. So if James had simply beckoned us to approach God, he would have been asking us to bridge the gap of sin—which is impossible. Also note: God is holy, absolutely pure, and will not draw near to sin. What is a person to do? James says, "Wash your hands, you sinners; purify your hearts, you hypocrites." In other words, you must become pure enough to satisfy God. But be honest—how good can you make yourself? Can you be as good as God?

The gospel is called the good news because it explains how a person can be good enough to please God. There is a very old prayer that has been preserved for us in the Episcopal Book of Common Prayer. Today, it is used regularly by believers who wish to figuratively wash their hands, actually purify their hearts, and draw near to God. Here is the prayer:

> *Most merciful God, we confess that we have*
> *sinned against you in thought, word, and deed,*
> *by what we have done, and by what we have*
> *left undone. We have not loved you with our*
> *whole heart; we have not loved our neighbors as*
> *ourselves. We are truly sorry and we humbly*
> *repent. For the sake of your Son Jesus Christ,*
> *have mercy on us and forgive us; that we may*
> *delight in your will, and walk in your ways, to*
> *the glory of your Name. Amen.* *

God, through the gospel of Jesus Christ, invites everyone to enter into the following contract: "If we say we have no sin, we are only fooling ourselves and refusing to accept the truth. But if we confess our sins to him, he is faithful and just to forgive us and to cleanse us from every wrong" (1 John 1:8–9). If you sincerely pray the old prayer quoted above, or any prayer similar to this, you fulfill your half of the gospel contract—you confess your sins. Then God completes the other half of the bargain by faithfully and justly forgiving you and cleansing you from all sin. Then you can come nearer, still nearer to God. That's a good deal.

* *The Book of Common Prayer.* New York: The Church Hymnal Corporation, 1979. p. 360.

Almighty God

have mercy on me,

forgive me all my sins

through my Lord Jesus Christ,

strengthen me in all goodness,

and by the power of the Holy Spirit

keep me in eternal life.

Amen. *

* Adapted from *The Book of Common Prayer*, p. 360.

The Lord is near

to all who call on him,

to all who call on him in truth.

PSALM 145:18 NRSV

O GOD, OUR HELP IN AGES PAST

Our God, our help in ages past,
Our hope for years to come,
Our shelter from the stormy blast,
And our eternal home.

Under the shadow of Thy throne
Thy saints have dwelt secure;
Sufficient is Thine arm alone,
And our defense is sure.

Before the hills in order stood,
Or earth received her frame,
From everlasting Thou art God,
To endless years the same.

Thy Word commands our flesh to dust,
"Return, ye sons of men:"
All nations rose from earth at first,
And turn to earth again.

A thousand ages in Thy sight
Are like an evening gone;
Short as the watch that ends the night
Before the rising sun.

The busy tribes of flesh and blood,
With all their lives and cares,
Are carried downwards by the flood,
And lost in following years.

Don't be drunk with wine,

because that will ruin your life.

Instead, let the Holy Spirit

fill and control you.

Then you will sing psalms and hymns

and spiritual songs among yourselves,

making music to the Lord in your hearts.

And you will always give thanks

for everything to God the Father

in the name of our Lord Jesus Christ.

EPHESIANS 5:18–20

There was a time in the English church when there were no hymns. Only psalms were sung during worship. Collected in a book called The Psalter, these were old and rather dreary. The church of the day believed that to use any words other than those of Scripture would be an insult to God. Then, in 1674, Isaac Watts was born the eldest son of a Congregationalist deacon. By the time the boy came of age, music in the church had reached its lowest ebb. As a child, Isaac Watts was a precocious literary genius who compulsively composed rhyming verse. So he was well prepared to lift English hymnody out of its doldrums, and this he did, creating lively versions of the psalms with meter and rhyme in the language of the New Testament. Many of these were published when Watts was only twenty-five years old. The churches in England at first resisted and ridiculed Watts's compositions, but when they were finally accepted, the name of Isaac Watts was permanently affixed to the English hymnal. In fact, during the eighteenth century, the hymnal was often simply called Watts.

Isaac Watts wrote about six hundred hymns. His best-known hymn is "Joy to the World," which he derived from Psalm 98. Another favorite is "Jesus Shall Reign," based on Psalm 72. The hymn "O God, Our Help In Ages Past," drawn from Psalm 90, is one of Watts's finest. Like Moses' psalm, it ponders the mystery of time. Since we live in a culture grasping for long life and captivated by youth and health and strength, we should pause and let Psalm 90 speak.

The psalm first places God outside of time, demonstrating that the divine is entirely different from the human:

> *Lord, through all the generations*
> *   you have been our home!*
> *Before the mountains were created,*
> *   before you made the earth and the world,*
> *   you are God, without beginning or end (vv. 1–2).*

In fact, God turns people back into dust, simply by saying, "Return to dust!" (v. 3). Years are but moments and people are as insubstantial as dreams or dry grass:

> *For you, a thousand years are as yesterday!*
> *   They are like a few hours!*
> *You sweep people away like dreams that disappear*
> *   or like grass that springs up in the morning.*
> *In the morning it blooms and flourishes,*
> *   but by evening it is dry and withered (vv. 4–6).*

The words are not only poetic, they are prophetic—
and prophecy can be cruelly honest. Take these lines for
example:

> *We live our lives beneath your wrath.*
> > *We end our lives with a groan.*
> *Seventy years are given to us!*
> > *Some may even reach eighty.*
> *But even the best of these years are filled with pain*
> > *and trouble; soon they disappear, and we are gone*
> > *(vv. 9–10).*

This psalm shows clearly that the message of the
Bible is not a feel-good, self-help program. Though it
does help us, its help comes in the living, healing light
of truth. So in the light of the truth of Psalm 90, let's
pray this prayer:

> *"Lord, remind me how brief my time on earth will be.*
> > *Remind me that my days are numbered,*
> > > *and that my life is fleeing away."*

PSALM 39:4

Teach us

to make the most of our time,

so that we may grow in wisdom.

PSALM 90:12

ROCK OF AGES

Rock of Ages, cleft for me,
Let me hide myself in Thee;
Let the water and the blood,
From Thy wounded side which flowed,
Be of sin the double cure;
Save from wrath and make me pure.

Not the labor of my hands
Can fulfill Thy law's demands;
Could my zeal no respite know,
Could my tears forever flow,
All for sin could not atone;
Thou must save, and Thou alone.

Simon Peter answered,

"You are the Messiah,

the Son of the living God."

Jesus replied, "You are blessed,

Simon son of John,

because my Father in heaven

has revealed this to you.

You did not learn this from any human being.

Now I say to you that you are Peter,

and upon this rock I will build my church,

and all the powers of hell

will not conquer it."

MATTHEW 16:16–18

The Scripture describes a rock that is a person. Its first appearance comes in Exodus 17:1–6 when the people of Israel came to a place in the desert called Rephidim. There was no water to be found there so the people complained to Moses, "Give us water to drink! . . .Why did you ever take us out of Egypt? Why did you bring us here? We, our children, and our livestock will all die!"

Moses pleaded with the Lord, "What should I do with these people? They are about to stone me!" The Lord told him, "Take your shepherd's staff. . .and walk on ahead of the people. I will meet you by the rock at Mount Sinai. Strike the rock, and water will come pouring out. Then the people will be able to drink." Moses did just as he was told; and water gushed out of the rock. This is the "Rock of Ages" described in Augustus Toplady's passionate hymn.

The cleaving of the rock at Mount Sinai is a crucial event in the history of faith. Later, as Israel wandered through the wilderness, they remembered that God was their rock (Psalm 78:35). You may ask, "Who says the rock is a person? And who is this person, anyway?" The apostle Paul answers these questions in a letter to the believers in the Greek city of Corinth:

I don't want you to forget, brothers and sisters,
God guided our ancestors in the wilderness long

ago by sending a cloud that moved ahead of them.
Remember that he brought them safely through
the waters of the sea on dry ground. This was
their baptism as followers of Moses, in the cloud
and the sea. All of them ate the same spiritual
food, and all of them drank the same spiritual
water; for they all drank from the spiritual rock
that traveled with them, and the rock was Christ
(1 Corinthians 10:1–4, author's paraphrase).

Figuratively speaking, the entire ancient nation of
Israel drank of the flow from Christ. We modern-day
believers do the same. The gospel tells the story:
When Jesus hung on the cross, the soldiers guarding
him saw that he was dead. And in what was intended
to be a final act of cruelty, one of the soldiers pierced
his side with a spear, and blood and water flowed out
(see John 19:33–35). I, for one, am unspeakably grateful, because now I can drink from the rock who is Jesus
Christ. And so can you.

Blood and water poured out of Jesus Christ that
long-ago day at Calvary. Here is the story of the blood:
Jesus and the disciples were together eating what was
to be Christ's final meal. Jesus took a loaf of bread and
asked God's blessing on it. Then he broke it into pieces
and gave it to the disciples, saying, "Take and eat this.
It is my body given for you. Do this in remembrance

of me." After supper he took a cup of wine, gave thanks, gave it to them and said, "Drink all of this wine. It is the token of my blood—the blood of the new covenant, which I will pour out to discharge the sins of many, which seals the covenant between God and his people. It is poured out to forgive the sins of many people" (see Matthew 26:19–28).

Dear Lord Jesus Christ,

you are the rock of my salvation,

the rock of ages.

I believe in you and am so grateful that

I can drink of all that has flowed out of you.

I drink of you by faith today, Lord Jesus,

and ask that you quench the soul-thirst

of people everywhere.

On the last day,

the climax of the festival,

Jesus stood and shouted to the crowds,

"If you are thirsty, come to me!

If you believe in me, come and drink!"

JOHN 7:37–38

FOR THE BEAUTY OF THE EARTH

For the beauty of the earth, for the glory of
the skies,
For the love which from our birth over and
around us lies.

Refrain
Lord of all, to thee we raise, this our hymn of
grateful praise.

For the beauty of each hour, of the day and of
the night,
Hill and vale, and tree and flower, sun and
moon, and stars of light.

For the joy of ear and eye, for the heart and
mind's delight,
For the mystic harmony linking sense to sound
and sight.

For the joy of human love, brother, sister,
parent, child,
Friends on earth and friends above, for all
gentle thoughts and mild.

From the time

the world was created,

people have seen the earth and sky

and all that God made.

They can clearly see his invisible qualities—

his eternal power and divine nature.

So they have no excuse whatsoever

for not knowing God.

ROMANS 1:20

How strange that people do not believe in God. The beauty of the earth and the glory of the skies testify that God exists. People know God through this testimony, yet they won't acknowledge God (see Romans 1:21–22).

The Bible has a quiz for people like this. It is found in Job, a book of the Old Testament that is among the masterpieces of world literature. The book is named after its central character, Job (pronounced *Joe* with a b-sound at the end), who attempts to understand the sufferings that engulf him. Its theme is the age-old problem of undeserved suffering. When Job questioned God about this dilemma, "the Lord answered Job from the whirlwind: 'Who is this that questions my wisdom with such ignorant words? Brace yourself, because I have some questions for you, and you must answer them' " (Job 38:1–3). Then follow four chapters of the most beautiful and meaningful poetry ever written.

Each of the verses are a challenge to those people who question God's motives or even God's very existence. The divine interrogator begins:

> *Where were you when I laid the foundation*
> *of the earth? Tell me, if you have understand-*
> *ing. Who determined its measurements—surely*
> *you know! Or who stretched the line upon it?*

*On what were its bases sunk, or who laid its
cornerstone when the morning stars sang together
and all the heavenly beings shouted for joy?*

JOB 38:4—7 NRSV

These questions seem impossible to answer. But
the answers are found all around everyone. "The heavens tell of the glory of God. The skies display his mar-
velous craftsmanship. Day after day they continue to
speak; night after night they make him known. They
speak without a sound or a word; their voice is silent
in the skies; yet their message has gone out to all the
earth, and their words to all the world (Psalm 19:1—4).
Job's divine interrogator asks him about the stars:

*Can you bind the chains of the Pleiades,
or loose the cords of Orion? Can you lead forth
the [Zodiac] in their season, or can you guide
the Bear with its children? Do you know the
ordinances of the heavens? Can you establish
their rule on the earth?*

*Shall a faultfinder contend with the
Almighty? Anyone who argues with God
must respond.*

JOB 38:31—33; 40:2 NRSV

The answer to each of these questions should be a humble "no." But humility equals weakness in modern life. Rather than admit ignorance, people choose to disregard the Creator and the eloquent questions of the book of Job.

> *Each hour of the day is filled with*
> *beauty, O Lord.*
> *The night, hills and valleys, the trees and flowers—*
> *each are filled with your loveliness.*
> *Thank you that the sun and moon*
> *and the stars light the earth.*
> *Lord of all, I raise to you this*
> *my prayer of grateful praise.*

Then Job replied to the Lord, "I am nothing—how could I ever find the answers? I will put my hand over my mouth in silence. I have said too much already. I have nothing more to say" (Job 40:3–5).

COME THOU ALMIGHTY KING

Come, Thou almighty King,
    Help us Thy name to sing, help us to praise!
Father all glorious, over all victorious,
    Come and reign over us, Ancient of Days!

Come, Thou incarnate Word,
    Gird on thy mighty sword, our prayer attend!
Come, and thy people bless, and give Thy
    Word success,
Spirit of holiness, on us descend!

Come, holy Comforter,
    Thy sacred witness bear in this glad hour.
Thou Who almighty art, now rule in every
    heart,
And ne'er from us depart, Spirit of power!

May the grace

of our Lord Jesus Christ,

the love of God,

and the fellowship

of the Holy Spirit

be with you all.

2 CORINTHIANS 13:13

This great hymn praises the one God who is mysteriously three. Note that the key word here is mysterious. The nature of God cannot be understood. Still there is a Christian doctrine of the Trinity that expresses the unity of Father, Son, and Holy Spirit in one Godhead. That is the topic of this hymn. So get ready because the next few paragraphs are going to describe this deep, vital point of the Christian faith.

The word Trinity does not appear in the New Testament, and there is no such doctrine expressly taught in Scripture. But the Christians who witnessed the coming of Jesus Christ also called him the Word. So their announcement of the gospel begins: "In the beginning the Word already existed. He was with God, and *he was God*" (John 1:1). Furthermore, Christ himself said, "I am in the Father and the Father is in me" (14:11).

Jesus told his disciples that although he was going away, the Holy Spirit would come to be with them forever. And he clearly identified his unity with the Spirit by saying, "I will not leave you orphaned; I am coming to you" (see John 14:15–18 NRSV).

The idea of this unity is strengthened in the Epistles. For example, 2 Corinthians 3:17 says, "The Lord is the Spirit." Verse 3:18 (NRSV) underlines this by saying that a believer's transformation comes "from the Lord, the Spirit."

The people of the early church were well aware that the Old Testament says, "Hear, O Israel: The Lord our God is one Lord" (Deuteronomy 6:4 RSV), and they did not reject this truth. Yet this one God had been clearly manifested as three: Father, Son, and Spirit. All three were associated as God in key passages of Scripture, such as the apostolic benediction in 2 Corinthians 13:14 and in Matthew 28:19—popularly known as the Great Commission: "Therefore, go and make disciples of all the nations, baptizing them in the name of the Father and the Son and the Holy Spirit."

The doctrine developed gradually and through much controversy until the fourth century when the Council of Nicaea assembled in A.D. 325. There the distinctness of the three and their unity were brought together in a single orthodox doctrine of one essence and three persons.

Now you may ask, "So what? This is for the theologians. Why does it matter to an ordinary believer?" There are a lot of reasons the doctrine of the Trinity is important. Here is just one: Our Savior Jesus is the eternal God because we need an eternal salvation. So the New Testament says, "There were many priests under the old [Jewish] system. When one priest died, another had to take his place. But Jesus remains a priest forever; his priesthood will never end. Therefore he is able, once and forever, to save everyone who comes to God through him. He lives forever to plead with God on their behalf" (Hebrews 7:23–25).

Remember, the nature of God is a mystery and cannot be understood by the creation. The Bible does not ask us to understand God, but expects that we will love God. So this great hymn about God's trinity concludes with a verse of love and praise:

To thee, great One-in-three,
 Eternal praises be, hence, evermore.
Thy sovereign majesty may we in glory see,
 And to eternity love and adore!

I bow my knees to you

dear Father and ask that you will

strengthen me in my inner being

through your Spirit,

and that Christ may dwell

in my heart through faith.

prayer adapted from EPHESIANS 3:14–16

ALL HAIL THE POWER OF JESUS' NAME

All hail the power of Jesus' Name! Let angels
    prostrate fall;
Bring forth the royal diadem, and crown Him
    Lord of all.
Bring forth the royal diadem, and crown Him
    Lord of all.

Ye chosen seed of Israel's race, ye ransomed
    from the fall,
Hail Him who saves you by his grace, and
    crown Him Lord of all.
Hail Him who saves you by his grace, and
    crown Him Lord of all.

Sinners, whose love can ne'er forget the worm-
    wood and the gall,
Go spread your trophies at His feet, and crown
    Him Lord of all.
Go spread your trophies at His feet, and crown
    Him Lord of all.

Let every kindred, every tribe on this terres-
    trial ball
To Him all majesty ascribe, and crown Him
    Lord of all.
To Him all majesty ascribe, and crown Him
    Lord of all.

Because of this,

God raised him up

to the heights of heaven

and gave him a name

that is above every other name,

so that at the name of Jesus

every knee will bow,

in heaven and on earth

and under the earth,

and every tongue will confess

that Jesus Christ is Lord,

to the glory of God the Father.

PHILIPPIANS 2:9–11

Here are some anecdotes from the life of Edward Perronet. First is the way he introduced his great hymn, "All Hail the Power of Jesus' Name," to the world. The first stanza appeared in The Gospel Magazine of November 1779. But no credit was given to Perronet. This magazine was edited by Augustus Toplady, author of "Rock of Ages." Five months later, the magazine published eight verses of this hymn under the title, "On the Resurrection, the Lord Is King." Again no author was given. Six months passed and the hymn resurfaced, again anonymously, but it was accompanied by an acrostic poem that revealed the hymn's author: The first letter of each line of the poem spelled "Edward Perronet." The last stanza of this hymn was added in 1887 by John Rippon, author of the hymn "How Firm a Foundation."

Perronet was descended from distinguished French Huguenots (Protestants) who fled the European continent to escape religious persecution. Like his father, Perronet was a priest in the Church of England although he once wrote, "I was born and I am likely to die in the tottering communion of the Church of England, but I despise her nonsense." Eventually, he quit and became a coworker of the evangelist John Wesley. At that time (the 1740s and 1750s), Wesley and his followers were subject to violent persecution. The following is a notation from Wesley's journal:

> *From Rockdale we went to Bolton, and soon found that the Rockdale lions were lambs in comparison with those of Bolton. Edward Perronet was thrown down and rolled in mud and mire. Stones were hurled and windows broken.*

Edward Perronet was eighteen years younger than John Wesley and stubbornly refused to preach when Wesley was present to do so. Still, Wesley, himself of strong will, regularly asked him to preach. One day he announced to a congregation that Perronet would preach at the next service. The younger man avoided a public conflict with Wesley and mounted the pulpit as scheduled. He explained that although he had never consented to preach, "I shall deliver the greatest sermon that has ever been preached on earth." He then read the Sermon on the Mount and sat down without comment.

With a strong mind and a free spirit, Perronet broke with Wesley over the issue of whether the Methodist evangelists could administer the sacraments.

Perronet wrote many other hymns and poems, most of which he published anonymously, but "All Hail the Power of Jesus' Name" is his only work to survive. He served an independent church in Canterbury, England, until his death. It is said that the following are the last words he uttered:

> *Glory to God in the height of his divinity!*
> *Glory to God in the depth of his humanity!*
> *Glory to God in his all-sufficiency!*
> *Into his hands I commend my spirit.*

He existed before

everything else began,

and he holds all creation together.

Christ is the head of the church,

which is his body.

He is the first of all

who will rise from the dead,

so he is first in everything.

For God in all his fullness

was pleased to live in Christ.

COLOSSIANS 1:17–19

Lord Jesus Christ,

I pray that Your

love and Your lordship

will fully infect my heart

that I give thanks, and sing,

and triumph forever.

Draw more people to love You

and rejoice in thanksgiving

that You are King!

Shout with joy

to the LORD, o earth!

Worship the LORD with gladness.

Come before him,

singing with joy.

PSALM 100:1–2

Inspirational Library

Beautiful purse/pocket-size editions of Christian classics bound in flexible leatherette. These books make thoughtful gifts for everyone on your list, including yourself!

When I'm on My Knees   The highly popular collection of devotional thoughts on prayer, especially for women.
    Flexible Leatherette. \$4.97

The Bible Promise Book   Over 1,000 promises from God's Word arranged by topic. What does God promise about matters like: Anger, Illness, Jealousy, Love, Money, Old Age, and Mercy? Find out in this book!
    Flexible Leatherette. \$3.97

Daily Wisdom for Women   A daily devotional for women seeking biblical wisdom to apply to their lives. Scripture taken from the New American Standard Version of the Bible.
    Flexible Leatherette. \$4.97

My Daily Prayer Journal   Each page is dated and features a Scripture verse and ample room for you to record your thoughts, prayers, and praises. One page for each day of the year.
    Flexible Leatherette. \$4.97

Available wherever books are sold.
Or order from:

Barbour Publishing, Inc.
P.O. Box 719
Uhrichsville, OH 44683
www.barbourbooks.com

If you order by mail, add \$2.00 to your order for shipping.
Prices are subject to change without notice.